If you want hours and hours of fun

AND

If you want to keep your friends in stitches—

YOU MUST TURN THE PAGES OF THIS BOOK. . .

The SUPER JOKE BOOK

By Gyles Brandreth

Illustrated by
Nick Berringer

STERLING

New York / London
www.sterlingpublishing.com/kids

STERLING and the distinctive Sterling logo are
registered trademarks of Sterling Publishing Co., Inc.

Library of Congress Cataloging-in-Publication Data

Brandreth, Gyles Daubeney, 1948-
The super joke book / by Gyles Brandreth ; illustrated by Nick
Berringer. -- Rev. ed.
p. cm.
Includes index.
ISBN 978-1-4027-4713-7 (pb-trade pbk. : alk. paper)
1. American wit and humor. 2. Wit and humor, Juvenile. I. Berringer,
Nick, ill. II. Title.
PN6163.B72 2009
818'.5402--dc22

2009014213

10 9 8 7 6 5
08/13

Published in 2009 by Sterling Publishing Co., Inc.
387 Park Avenue South, New York, NY 10016.
Material in this book was previously published by Sterling in 1985
using material compiled from *1000 Jokes: The Greatest Joke Book Ever Known*,
published in Great Britain by Carousel Books, a division of Transworld
Publishers Ltd.

Distributed in Canada by Sterling Publishing
c/o Canadian Manda Group, 165 Dufferin Street Toronto,
Ontario, Canada M6K 3H6

Manufactured in the United States of America

Sterling ISBN 978-1-4027-4713-7

For information about custom editions, special sales, premium and
corporate purchases, please contact Sterling Special Sales Department
at 800-805-5489 or specialsales@sterlingpublishing.com.

Contents

1

Off & Running

BARNEY: I've owned this car for fifteen years and never had a wreck.

PROSPECTIVE BUYER: You mean you've owned this wreck for fifteen years and never had a car.

MOTHER: Bobby's teacher said he ought to have an encyclopedia.

FATHER: Let him walk to school like I had to.

REGGIE: We've got a new dog—would you like to come around and play with him?
RON: Well, I don't know—does he bite?
REGGIE: That's what I want to find out.

"Doctor, I keep thinking I'm a goat."
"How long have you had this feeling?"
"Ever since I was a kid."

MOTHER: Why are you keeping this box of dirt, Willy?
WILLY: That's instant mud-pie mix.

BOY (*howling*): A crab just bit my toe.
FATHER: Which one?
BOY: How should I know? All crabs look alike to me.

SAFECRACKER: I think I need glasses.
MATT: How's that?
SAFECRACKER: Well, I was twirling the knobs of a safe and an orchestra began to play.

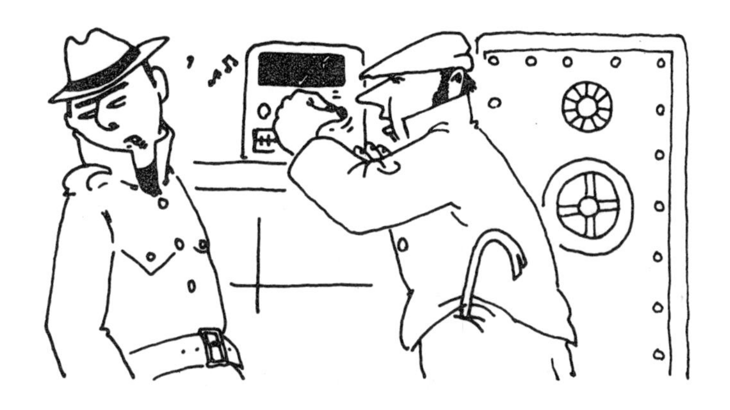

BOSS *(to department head)*: How many people work in your office?
DEPARTMENT HEAD: About half of them, sir.

"Why are you scratching yourself, Mary?"
"Because nobody else knows where I itch."

DOCTOR: Good morning, Mrs. Potter, I haven't seen you for a long time.
MRS. POTTER: I know, Doctor, I've been ill.

WAITER: How did you find your chop, sir?
DINER: I looked under a French fry and there it was!

TEACHER: Why do we sometimes call the Middle Ages the Dark Ages?
BETTY: Because they had so many knights.

A little boy saw a grass snake for the first time.
"Mother," he cried, "here's a tail without a body."

TEACHER: Polly, how can you prove the world is round?
POLLY: I never said it was.

A little boy and an old man were standing in the aisle of a crowded bus.

"Pass farther down the bus," called the conductor.

"He's not my father," the boy shouted back, "he's my grandfather."

CAPTAIN: Why didn't you stop the ball?
GOALIE: I thought that's what the nets were for.

FRANKIE: Which month has twenty-eight days?
PEGGY: All of them.

MIKE: I saw all your chickens out in your front yard yesterday.
PATRICK: Yes, they heard that men were coming to lay a sidewalk, and they wanted to see how it was done.

MOTHER: Bobby, have you given the goldfish fresh water today?
BOBBY: No, they haven't finished what I gave them yesterday.

TOMMY: Dad, what are four grapes and three grapes?
DAD: Don't you know simple arithmetic? Haven't you done a problem like that before?
TOMMY: No, Dad, we always use bananas at school.

"Doctor—I can't get to sleep at night."
"Don't worry—just lie on the edge of the bed and soon you'll drop off."

"Waiter, there's a dead fly in my soup."
"Yes, sir, I know—it's the heat that kills them."

BIG MAN (*in a theater, to a small boy sitting behind him*): Can you see, sonny?
BOY: No, sir, not at all.
BIG MAN: Then just watch me and laugh when I do.

Did you hear the one about the cornflakes?
I can only tell you a little at a time—it's a serial.

Two fleas were leaving the movie theater and one said to the other: "Shall we walk or take a dog?"

MRS. JONES: Will you join me in a cup of tea?
MRS. SMITH: I don't think there's room in there for both of us.

BETTY: That man next door has carrots growing in his ears.
HAROLD: How terrible!
BETTY: It certainly is. He planted turnips.

"Did you know that deep breathing kills germs?"
"Yes, but how do you get them to breathe deeply?"

NURSE: Well, Mr. Smith, you seem to be coughing much more easily this morning.
MR. SMITH: That's because I've been practicing all night.

"My uncle has 500 men under him."
"He must be very important."
"Actually, he's a maintenance man in a cemetery."

DENTIST: Please stop howling. I haven't even touched your tooth yet.
PATIENT: I know, but you're standing on my foot.

TEACHER: Mary, can you name four animals of the cat family?
MARY: Mother cat, father cat, and two kittens.

Advertisement in local paper:

LOST—WRISTWATCH BY A LADY
WITH A CRACKED FACE

BOBBY: Dad, I'm too tired to do my homework.

DAD: Now, my boy, hard work never killed anyone yet.

BOBBY: Well, I don't want to run the risk of being the first.

TEACHER: Sidney, can you tell me how fast light travels?

SIDNEY: I don't know, but it always gets here too early in the morning.

TEACHER: Brown, stop talking. Do you think you're the teacher of this class?

BROWN: No, sir.

TEACHER: Right, then stop behaving like a fool.

CUSTOMER: Waiter, I've only got one piece of meat.

WAITER: Just a moment, sir, and I'll cut it in two.

Little Bernie was taking his new dog for a walk when a policeman stopped him.

"Has your dog got a license?" the policeman asked.

"Oh, no," answered Bernie. "He's not old enough to drive."

PAT: I didn't sleep well last night.
MATT: Why was that?
PAT: I plugged the electric blanket into the toaster by mistake and kept popping out of bed all night.

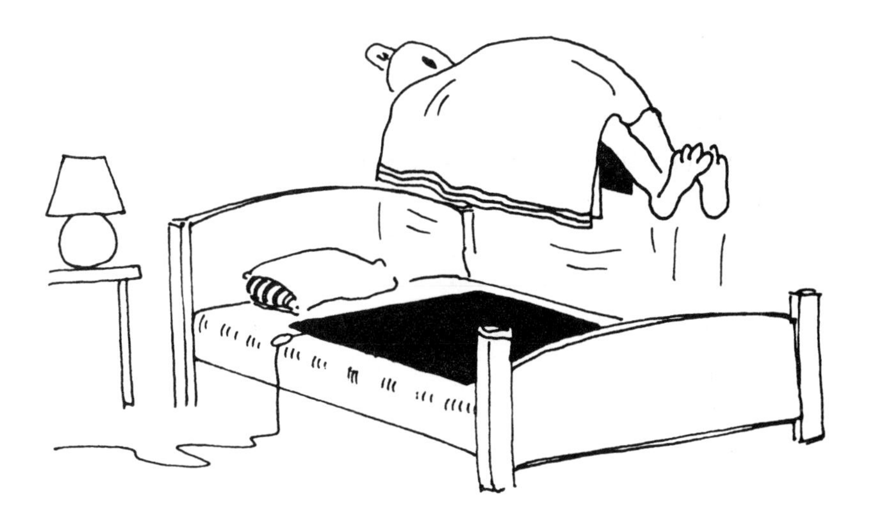

ANGRY BOSS *(to office boy)*: You're late again this morning.

OFFICE BOY: I overslept.

ANGRY BOSS: You mean you sleep at home, *too?*

"Will the band play anything I ask them to?"
"Certainly, sir."
"Well, ask them to play chess."

FATHER: Freddie, you're a pig. Do you know what a pig is?

FREDDIE: Sure, Dad. A pig is a hog's little boy.

NURSE: Can I take your pulse?

PATIENT: Why? Haven't you got one of your own?

MOTHER LION: Son, what are you doing?
BABY LION: I am chasing a man around a tree.
MOTHER LION: How often must I tell you not to play with your food!

CUSTOMER (*in butcher shop*): Have you got a sheep's head?
BUTCHER: No, it's just the way I part my hair.

HOTEL RECEPTIONIST IN FRANCE (*to tourist*): Are you a foreigner?
TOURIST: Certainly not! I'm from the good old U.S. of A!

"Would you like to buy a pocket calculator, sir?"
"No, thanks, I know how many pockets I've got."

A tourist visiting New York saw a restaurant that claimed it could supply any dish ordered, so he asked the waiter for kangaroo on toast.

After a while the waiter came back and said, "I'm so sorry, sir, but we've run out of bread."

DON: Why did Ron sleep under the oil tank last night?

JOHN: Because he wanted to get up oily in the morning.

VISITOR: Is this a healthy place to live?

LOCAL YOKEL: Yes, sir, when I arrived here I couldn't walk or eat solid food.

VISITOR: What was the matter with you?

LOCAL YOKEL: Nothing—I was born here.

"The opening is for a garbage collector. Have you any experience?"

"No, but I'll pick it up as I go along."

2

Bad News!

SUSIE: Mother, what was the name of the last station our train stopped at?

MOTHER: I don't know—can't you see I'm reading?

SUSIE: Well, it's too bad, because that's where little Benny got off.

WIFE: Do you have a good memory for faces?

HUSBAND: Yes—why?

WIFE: I just broke your shaving mirror.

MOTORIST: When I bought this car you said it was rust-free, but the underneath is covered with it.
DEALER: Yes, sir. The car's rust-free. We didn't charge for it.

Did you hear the one about the man who always wore sunglasses?
He took a dim view of things.

TEACHER: Bobby, can you name the four seasons?
BOBBY: Salt, pepper, vinegar, and mustard.

SERGEANT (*to new recruit*): What were you before you joined the army?
NEW RECRUIT: Happy, Sergeant.

TEACHER: Which is farther away, Australia or the moon?
BOBBY: Australia.
TEACHER: Why do you say that?
BOBBY: We can see the moon, and we can't see Australia.

Should you stir your tea with your left hand or your right hand?
Neither—use your spoon.

JUDGE: I don't understand why you broke into the same store three nights in a row.

PRISONER: Well, Your Honor, I picked out a dress for my wife, and I had to exchange it twice.

HARRY: This lamb is very tough.

POLLY: I'm sorry—the butcher said it was spring lamb.

HARRY: Well, I must be eating one of the springs.

PETER: My teacher was mad because I didn't know where the pyramids were.

MOTHER *(absently)*: Well, dear, next time remember where you put things.

MOVIE ATTENDANT: That's the sixth ticket you've bought.

CUSTOMER: I know—there's a woman in there who keeps tearing them up.

"My husband is so ugly that when he goes to the zoo he has to buy two tickets—one to get in and one to get out."

"This pair of shoes you sold me yesterday is ridiculous. One of them has a heel two inches shorter than the other. What am I supposed to do?"
"Limp."

MR. JOHNSON: Are you using your mower this afternoon?
MR. SMITH: Yes.
MR: JOHNSON: Fine. Then can I borrow your tennis racket, since you won't be needing it?

SALLY: Did you see the guards change while you were in London?
LULU: No, they always pulled the blinds down.

CUSTOMER: You said this simple gadget was foolproof. I can't see how to use it.
SHOPKEEPER: Then it's what it says it is. It proves you're a fool.

"Why are you jumping up and down?"
"I've just taken some medicine and I forgot to shake the bottle."

WRITER: I took up writing full-time a year ago.
FRIEND: Have you sold anything?
WRITER: Yes—my TV, all the furniture, the house . . . .

It's easy to make time fly. Just throw an alarm clock over your shoulder.

"I've never been troubled with backseat drivers."
"Why, what car do you drive?"
"A hearse."

A woman dashed into a hardware store and asked to be served at once.

"Give me a mousetrap, please," she gasped. "I've got to catch a train."

"I'm sorry," said the clerk. "We haven't got anything as big as that."

MOTHER: Freddie, why is your face so red?
FREDDIE: I was running up the street to stop a fight.
MOTHER: That's a very nice thing to do. Who was fighting?
FREDDIE: Jackie Smith and I.

TEACHER: Now, Jackie, what is the highest form of animal life?
JACKIE: I think it's the giraffe.

"Why were you driving so fast?" the policeman asked the speeding motorist.

"Well, my brakes are no good, and I wanted to get home before I had an accident."

A guide was showing Niagara Falls to a man from Texas.

GUIDE: I'll bet you don't have anything like this in Texas.

TEXAN: Nope, but in Texas we have plumbers who can fix it.

How can you decide whether to use a screw or a nail when doing carpentry?

Drive in a nail—if the wood splits, you should have used a screw.

A man was driving the wrong way down a one-way street. He was stopped by a policeman.

"This is a one-way street," said the officer.

"I know," said the motorist, "I'm only going one way."

SALESMAN: Little boy, is your mother home?
WILLIE: Yes, sir.
SALESMAN (*after knocking and knocking with no reply*): I thought you said your mother was home.
WILLIE: She is, but we don't live here.

JUDGE: Tell me, why did you park your car here?
MOTORIST: Well, there was a sign that said "Fine for Parking."

Due to a strike at the meteorological office, there will be no weather tomorrow.

"I went to the dentist this morning."
"Does your tooth still hurt'?"
"I don't know—the dentist kept it."

"Do you write with your left hand or your right hand?"
"Neither—I write with a ballpoint pen."

A beautiful young lady kissed a prince last night—and he turned into a frog.

WOMAN: *(on phone)*: Doctor, what can I do? My little boy has swallowed my pen!
DOCTOR: Use a pencil.

A schoolboy took a book out of the library. The cover read "How to Hug." He discovered to his disappointment that it was volume 7 of the encyclopedia.

"My dog has no nose."
"How does it smell?"
"Terrible."

Charlie ate too many jam tarts. He clutched his stomach and groaned.
"Are you in pain?" asked his mother.
"No," moaned Charlie, "the pain's in me."

DOORMAN: Your car is at the door, sir.
CAR OWNER: Yes, I can hear it knocking.

WAITER: And what will you have, sir, after the steak?
DINER: Indigestion, I expect.

3

Funny Folks

"Every day my dog and I go for a tramp in the woods."

"Does the dog enjoy it?"

"Oh, yes—but the tramp is a bit fed up."

"I hear you've fallen in love with Dracula."

"Yes, it was love at first bite."

MOTHER: Now, Monty, you know you're not supposed to eat with your knife.
MONTY: I know, Ma, but my fork leaks.

BETTY: I had a fall last night that left me unconscious for eight hours.
HETTY: How dreadful! Where did you fall?
BETTY: I fell asleep.

YOUNG MAN: Er, excuse me—but would you go out with me tonight?
DOLLY: Oh, I don't go out with perfect strangers.
YOUNG MAN: I never said I was perfect!

DOCTOR: How are you now, Mr. Gibson, after your heart operation?
MR. GIBSON: Well, Doctor, I'm fine, but I seem to have two heartbeats.
DOCTOR: Oh, dear, I wondered where my wristwatch had gone.

MO: Where do you weigh whales?
JO: I don't know.
MO: At a whale weigh station, of course!

PATIENT: Will my measles be better next week, doctor?

DOCTOR: I don't like to make rash promises.

CUSTOMER *(to bank manager)*: Will you help me out, please?

BANK MANAGER: Certainly—go through that door.

MAN *(on telephone to weather bureau)*: What are the chances of a shower today?

WEATHERMAN: It's okay with me, sir. If you want one, take one.

GUIDE *(on safari)*: Quick, sir, shoot that leopard right on the spot.

LORD CLARENCE: Be specific, man, which spot?

CUSTOMER: Waiter, please bring me coffee without cream.

WAITER: I'm afraid we've run out of cream. Would you like it without milk?

OLD MAN *(to his wife)*: What on earth are you doing?

WIFE: Knitting up some barbed-wire fence.

OLD MAN: How can you do that?

WIFE: I'm using steel wool.

TEACHER: I wish you'd pay a little attention.
ANGIE: I'm paying as little as I can.

After the dance, the young man asked the young lady if he could see her home—so she showed him a photograph of it.

BERT: Mom, there's a man with a bill at the door.
MOMMY: Don't be silly, dear, it must be a duck with a hat on.

BRIGHT BILLY: Dad, is your watch going?
DAD: Yes, of course it is.
BRIGHT BILLY: Then when's it coming back?

STARTER (*at boat race*): Come in, Number 9—your time is up.
ASSISTANT: But we've only got eight boats.
STARTER: Are you in trouble, Number 6?

In Dodge City the Sheriff arrested Lulu Belle for wearing a taffeta dress.

"What's the charge, Sheriff?" she asked.

"Rustlin', of course," he replied.

TOMMY: Are worms good to eat?
DAD: I shouldn't think so. Why?
TOMMY: There was one in your pie.

Why do cows in Switzerland have bells around their necks?

Because their horns don't work.

4

Surprise!

DAN: When I grow up, I'm going to be a policeman and follow in my father's footsteps.

STAN: I didn't know your father was a policeman.

DAN: He's not—he's a burglar.

MR. BROWN: I've noticed Mr. Johnson's manners have improved lately.

MRS. BROWN: Yes, he got a job in a refinery.

PATIENT: What can you give me for flat feet, Doctor?

DOCTOR: Have you tried a bicycle pump?

Goofy Gus went into a shop with a small pie stuck in each ear.

"Excuse me," said the salesclerk, "but you've got small pies in your ears."

"You'll have to speak up," said Goofy Gus. "I've got small pies in my ears."

POSTMAN: I have a parcel here, but the name on it is obliterated.

JACKSON: Can't be for me, then. My name's Jackson.

The poet had been droning on at the party about his various sources of inspiration.

"Yes," he told the young woman, "I'm at present collecting some of my better poems to be published posthumously."

"Lovely," said the woman. "I'll look forward to it."

Harry and Larry were given a toboggan for Christmas. After they had been out playing in the snow, Larry was in tears.

"Now, Harry," said his father, "I told you to let Larry use the toboggan half the time."

"And I did," said Harry. "He had it going up, and I had it going down."

"Is your new horse well-behaved?"
"Oh, yes. When we come to a fence, he stops and lets me go over first."

HUSBAND: What would you like for your birthday?
WIFE: Oh—let it be a surprise.
HUSBAND: Right . . . BOO!

JILL: Daddy, Jack's broken my new doll.
DADDY: How did he do that?
JILL: I hit him on the head with it.

Little Caroline was drawing a Nativity picture—there were Mary and Joseph, shepherds and wise men.

"What's that in the corner?" asked her teacher.

"That's their TV, of course," replied Caroline.

Dolphins are so intelligent that within a few weeks of captivity they can train a man to stand on the edge of their pool and throw them fish three times a day.

MOTHER: Did you behave well in church today, Margie?

MARGIE: I certainly did. A nice man offered me a plate full of money, and I said, "No, thank you."

TEACHER: Now, Brenda, how many fingers do you have?
BRENDA: Ten.
TEACHER: Right. Now if you lost four of them in an accident, what would you have?
BRENDA: No more piano lessons.

FRIEND: And what are you going to give your baby brother for his birthday, Janet?
JANET: I don't know—last year I gave him measles.

Young Tim was raking leaves with his father, who was telling him about how the fairies turned the leaves brown. He looked up pityingly at his father.

"Haven't you ever heard of photosynthesis?" he asked.

What does 36 inches make in Glasgow?

One Scotland Yard.

The visitor stared in amazement at the child hammering nails into the posh Scandinavian furniture.

He turned to his host. "Don't you find it expensive to let your son play games like that?" he asked.

"Not really," replied the host. "I get the nails wholesale."

A policeman saw an old man pulling a box on a leash down a busy street.

"Poor man," he thought. "I'd better humor him."

"That's a nice dog you've got there," he said to the old man.

"It isn't a dog, it's a box," said the old man.

"Oh, I'm sorry," said the policeman, "I thought you were a bit confused," and he walked on.

The old man turned and looked at the box.

"We fooled him that time, Rover," he said.

POLICEMAN: I'm sorry, Sonny, but you need a permit to fish here.

SONNY: That's all right, thanks. I'm doing okay with a worm.

NEW HUSBAND: Just think, darling—we've now been married for twenty-four hours!

NEW WIFE: Yes, darling, and it seems like only yesterday.

GORDON: How's your sister doing with her reducing diet?

CHARLIE: Fine—she disappeared last week.

MORRIS: Can you spell blind pig?

NORMAN: B-l-i-n-d p-i-g.

MORRIS: No. It's b-l-n-d p-g. With two i's, he wouldn't be blind.

Sign in a police station:

IT TAKES ABOUT 3500 BOLTS TO PUT A CAR TOGETHER BUT ONLY ONE NUT TO SCATTER IT ALL OVER THE ROAD.

5

Excuse Me!

Goofy Gus took a friend driving on a narrow mountain road.

After a while the friend said, "I feel very scared whenever you go around one of those sharp bends."

"Then do what I do," said Gus, "close your eyes."

MOTHER: Why is your little brother crying?
BILLY: Because I won't give him my piece of cake.
MOTHER: Is his piece gone?
BILLY: Yes—he cried when I ate that, too.

"Our next comedian is so bad that when he took part in an outdoor show in the park, twenty-six trees got up and walked out."

FATHER (*at breakfast*): My goodness, son, that was some thunderstorm we had last night.
SON: It certainly was.
MOTHER: Oh, dear, why didn't you wake me up? You know I can't sleep in a thunderstorm.

CUSTOMER: Those sausages you sold me were meat at one end and bread at the other.
BUTCHER: Yes, ma'am, in these times, it's difficult to make both ends meat.

CUSTOMER: I found a fly in one of those raisin buns you sold me yesterday.
SHOP OWNER: Well, bring it back and I'll exchange it for a raisin.

MAN (*to psychiatrist*): I'm worried—I keep thinking I'm a pair of curtains.
PSYCHIATRIST: Stop worrying and pull yourself together.

Simple Simon went to buy a pillowcase.
"What size?" said the clerk.
"I don't know," said Simon.
"But I wear a seven-and-a-half hat."

JINKS: I notice your neighbor doesn't let his chickens run loose any more. Why is that?
BINKS: Well, I hid six eggs under a bush the other night. Next day I made sure he saw me collect the eggs.

A young lady went into a bank to withdraw some money.

"Can you identify yourself?" asked the clerk.

The young lady opened her handbag, took out a mirror, looked into it and said, "Yes, it's me, all right."

PIANO TUNER: I've come to tune your piano.
PIANO OWNER: But we didn't send for you.
PIANO TUNER: No, but your neighbors did.

YOUNG MAN: I've come to ask for your daughter's hand.
FATHER: You'll have to take all of her or it's no deal.

The medical lecturer turned to one of his students and said, "Now, Merryweather, it is clear from this X-ray that one of this patient's legs is much shorter than the other. This accounts for the patient's limp. But what would you do in a case like this?"

Merryweather thought for a moment, then said brightly, "Well, sir, I should imagine that I would limp, too."

Sammy had been on an outing with his father.

"Well," said his mother, when they got home, "did you like the zoo?"

"Oh, it was fine," replied Sammy. "And Dad liked it, too—especially when one of the animals came racing to the finish line."

NEWS BROADCAST: Two prisoners escaped today from Wakefield prison. One is seven feet tall and the other is four feet six. The police are hunting high and low for them.

BROWN: The police are looking for a man with one eye called Smith.

WHITE: What's his other eye called?

CLOAKROOM ATTENDANT: Please leave your hat here, sir.

CLUB CUSTOMER: I haven't got a hat.

CLOAKROOM ATTENDANT: Then I'm afraid you can't come into the club. My orders are that people cannot enter unless they leave their hats in the cloakroom.

A woman decided to breed chickens, but she didn't have much luck. At last, she wrote to the Department of Agriculture for some advice.

She wrote: "Every morning I find one or two of my prize chickens lying stiff and cold on the ground with their legs in the air. Would you kindly tell me what is the matter?"

A few days later she got this reply: "Your chickens are dead."

BARRY: How many balls of string would it take to reach the moon?

LARRY: Only one—if it were long enough.

GREEDY BOY: I got through a jar of jam today.

FRIEND: It must have been a tight squeeze.

FIRST BIRD *(to his friend)*: Look, there's a jumbo jet. I wish I could go as fast as that.
SECOND BIRD: You could, if your bottom were on fire.

POLLY: What's the weather like?
MOLLY: I don't know—it's so cloudy I can't see.

GRANDMA: I like to go to bed and get up with the chickens, don't you?
BETTY: No, I like to sleep in my own bed.

NED: What goes ninety-nine bump, ninety-nine bump, ninety-nine bump?
ED: A centipede with a wooden leg.

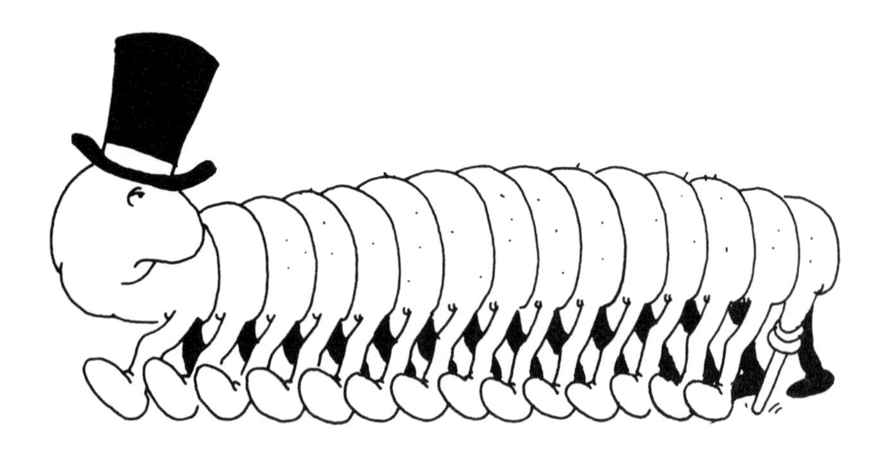

OLD SALT: I had a parrot for five years and it never said a word.
YOUNG SAILOR: It must have been tongue-tied.
OLD SALT: No, it was stuffed.

MOLLY: Did you hear the one about the bed?
POLLY: No.
MOLLY: It hasn't been made up yet.

"Why are you drinking blue and white paint?"
"Because I'm an interior decorator."

ROGER: Your overcoat is very loud.
RODNEY: It's not so bad when I put on a muffler.

JUDGE: I shall give you a short sentence.
PRISONER: Thank you, Your Honor
JUDGE: Ten years.
PRISONER: Ten years—that's not a short sentence!
JUDGE: Yes, it is—it's two words.

"Waiter, there's a button in my salad."
"Oh, it must have come off when the salad was dressing."

A man bought a grandfather clock from an antique shop. In the street he put it over his shoulder, and as he did so, knocked over a woman on the street.

"Fool," she yelled, "why can't you wear a wristwatch like the rest of us?"

"Why did Harold leave his job?"
"Illness."
"Anything serious?"
"Yes. The boss got sick of him."

PATIENT: If I take these little blue pills, as you suggest, will I get better?

DOCTOR: Well, put it this way—none of my patients has ever come back to ask for more.

"Doctor, I feel like a pack of cards."
"Wait over there, I'll deal with you later."

WAITER: We have practically everything on the menu.
DINER: So I see—would you bring me a clean one, please?

A visitor was being shown around a farm, when he saw a bull in a field.

He called out, "Is that bull safe?"

"Well," said the farmer, "offhand I'd say he's a lot safer than you are."

FRED: What is the noblest dog?
NED: The hot dog—it feeds the hand that bites it.

After robbing the bank, the thief rushed home and began to saw the legs off his bed. His wife asked him what he was doing.

"I want to lie low for a while," he explained.

HETTY: My doctor put me on a diet with more corn and vegetable oils.
BETTY: Does it work?
HETTY: I don't know yet. I'm not thinner, but I don't squeak anymore.

MOTHER: Willy, it's rude to keep stretching across the table for the cake. Haven't you got a tongue?

WILLY: Yes, but my arm's longer.

BOSS: Look at all the dust on this desk. It looks as if it hasn't been cleaned for a month and a half.

EMPLOYEE: Don't blame me, sir, I've only been here a week.

6

How Odd . . .

Three rather deaf old friends met one day.

"Windy, isn't it?" said one.

"No, it's Thursday," said the second.

"So am I," said the third. "Let's go and have a cup of coffee."

FIRST PATIENT: I see they've brought in another case of tonsillitis.

SECOND PATIENT: Anything is better than that lousy lemonade they've been giving us lately.

WRITER: You know, it took me over twenty years to find out I have no writing ability.
ACQUAINTANCE: So what did you do—give it up?
WRITER: Oh, no, by then I was so famous I couldn't afford to.

Newton discovered gravity when an apple hit him on the head.

He was shaken to the core.

LADY (*dialing 911*): Help! Please come to my house at once!
POLICEMAN: What's the trouble, lady?
LADY: That dreadful new postman is sitting up in a tree in my front yard, teasing my dog.

MAN: My dog has no tail.
FRIEND: Then how do you know when he's happy?
MAN: Oh, he stops biting me.

BEN: I hear the workers are striking for shorter hours.
LEN: Good thing, too—I always did think sixty minutes was too long for an hour.

HUSBAND: I've just discovered oil.
WIFE: Wonderful. Now we can get a new car.
HUSBAND: We'd better get the old one fixed first—that's where the oil's coming from.

JUDGE: As the jury has found you not guilty of fraud, you are now free to go.
PRISONER: Does that mean I can keep the money?

After class, the absentminded professor asked if anybody had seen his coat.

"You have it on, sir," he was told.

"Oh, thank you very much," he replied. "Otherwise, I might have gone off without it."

Silly Billy came home from the railway station complaining that he felt ill because he had been riding backward for three hours on the train.

"Why didn't you ask the person sitting opposite you to change seats?" his mother asked.

"I couldn't," he said. "There wasn't anybody sitting opposite me."

A little boy noticed some green parakeets in a pet shop.

"Look, Mommy," he said, "there are some canaries that aren't ripe."

BILL: Do you have holes in your trousers?
JIM: Certainly not.
BILL: Then how do you get your legs through?

WOMAN *(visiting artist in his studio)*: Do you like painting people in the nude?
ARTIST: No, personally I prefer painting with my clothes on.

FRANK: Four sailors fell in the sea, but only one of them got his hair wet.
JOHNNY: How was that?
FRANK: Three of them were bald.

VISITOR *(at gate)*: Does your dog bite strangers?
MAN: Only when he doesn't know them.

The professor was checking papers in his study when his telephone rang. His secretary answered it.

"Long distance from New York," she said.

"Yes, I know," answered the professor.

Dying words of a famous Chicago gangster: "Who put that violin in my violin case?"

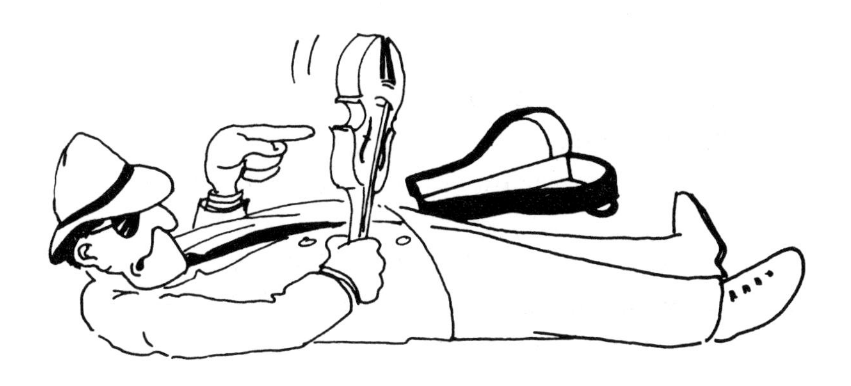

TEACHER: Now can somebody tell me where elephants are found?
MARY: Well, elephants are so big they are hardly ever lost.

MRS. GREEN: I see you and your husband are taking French lessons—why is that?
MRS. BLACK: We've adopted a French baby, and we want to be able to understand him as soon as he learns to talk.

The professor looked at one of his students.

"Don't you have a brother who took this course last year?" he asked.

"No, sir," said the student. "I'm just taking it again."

"My word," said the professor, "amazing resemblance."

What did the penny say when it got stuck in the slot?

"Money's very tight these days."

TEACHER *(on phone)*: You say Tommy has a cold and can't come to school? To whom am I speaking?
VOICE: This is my father.

RON: You dance beautifully.
JEAN: I wish I could say the same for you.
RON: You could—if you were as big a liar as I am.

ADAM: And I shall call that creature over there a rhinoceros.
EVE: But why call it that?
ADAM: Because it looks like a rhinoceros.

If at first you don't succeed, you're just like 99.9 percent of the population.

JACKIE: I wouldn't marry you if you were the last person on earth.
JOHNNY: If I were, you wouldn't be here.

VISITOR: And how do you like going to school, Willie?
WILLIE: I like going, and I like coming back. It's the bit in between I don't like.

WAITER: Yes, sir, you can have anything you see on the menu.
DINER: Well, how about dirty finger marks, grease stains, and gravy—in that order.

LARGE WOMAN: I'm very annoyed with that scale.

FRIEND: Why's that?

LARGE WOMAN: When I stepped on it, it said, "One person at a time, please."

How do we know that Moses wore a wig?
Because sometimes he was seen with Aaron and sometimes without.

TAD: How do fishermen make their nets, Dad?

DAD: Easy. They just take a lot of holes and sew them together.

Wholesome—the only thing from which you can take the whole and still have some left.

Sarah hadn't been paying attention when the teacher was explaining the importance of milk.

When the teacher asked her to name six things with milk in them, she thought for a moment.

Then she said, "Hot chocolate, ice cream, rice pudding, and three cows."

"My mother-in-law has gone to Indonesia."
"Jakarta?"
"No, she went by plane."

7

Oh, No!

Two little boys were looking at an abstract painting in an art shop.

"Let's run," said one, "before they say we did it."

MUGGER: Will you give me your money or shall I shoot you?

BURT: Shoot me. I need the money for my old age.

"Your money or your life," said the mugger to the miser.

When there was no reply, he repeated the demand. "Come on, man, your money or your life, which will it be?"

"Quiet," said the miser, "I'm thinking about it."

WALTER: A steamroller ran over my uncle.

RICHARD: What did you do?

WALTER: I took him home and slipped him under the door.

A man came back to the dealer from whom he bought a new car.

"I believe you gave me a guarantee with my car," he said.

"That's right, sir," the dealer answered. "We will replace anything that breaks."

"Fine. I need a new garage door."

CUSTOMER: I'd like to try on that dress in the window.

SALESLADY: I'm sorry, ma'am, you'll have to use the fitting room like everybody else.

DOCTOR: Mrs. Smith, you have acute bronchitis.

PATIENT: I came here to be examined, not admired.

MILLY: Do you have hot water at your house?
BILLY: We sure do. And I'm always in it.

SUZIE: I'd like two ounces of bird seed, please.
PET SHOP OWNER: How many birds have you, dear?
SUZIE: None right now, but I want to grow some.

A lady went to buy some wool to knit a sweater for her dog.

"Perhaps you'd better bring him in," said the saleslady. "Then I can tell you how much wool to buy."

"Oh, no," said the customer, "it's supposed to be a surprise!"

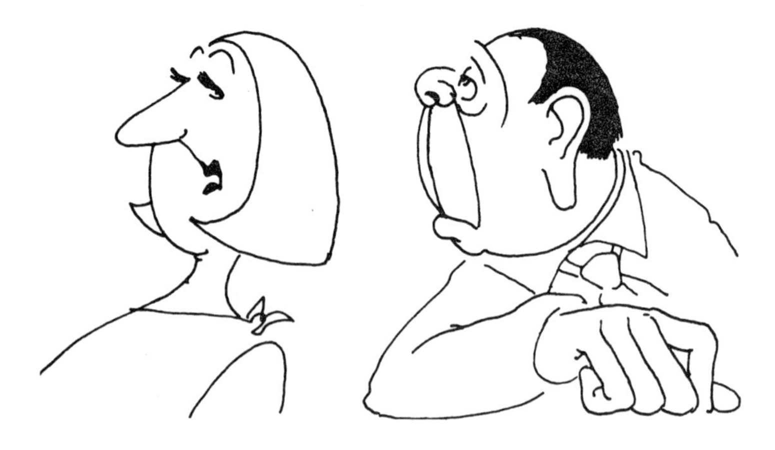

"Darling, you have the face of a saint."
"Thank you, darling, which saint?"
"A Saint Bernard."

CUSTOMER: Can this wool coat be worn in wet weather?
CLERK: Madam, have you ever seen a sheep carry an umbrella?

A man came to the police station and complained, "I've got three brothers—we all live in one room. One of my brothers has six cats, another has five dogs, and the other has a goat. The smell is terrible. Can you do something about it?"

"Well, why don't you open the windows?" asked the policeman.

"What? And lose all my pigeons?"

PROUD MOTHER: My baby is a year old now, and he's been walking since he was eight months old.
BORED VISITOR: Really? He must be awfully tired.

Percival was so wealthy that even the bags under his eyes had his initials on them.

"Doctor, you remember last year you told me to stay away from dampness if I wanted my rheumatism to get better?"
"Yes," said the doctor.
"Well, it's better. Is it all right for me to take a bath now?"

A beginning rider at the stables was trying to saddle a horse.

"Excuse me," said the old hand, "but you're putting that saddle on backward."

"How do you know," snapped the beginner. "You don't know which way I'm going."

Keep smiling—it makes everyone wonder what you're up to.

TOURIST: Whose skull is that?

TIRED GUIDE: That, sir, is the skull of Julius Caesar.

TOURIST: Then whose is that small one beside it?

TIRED GUIDE: That, sir, is the skull of Julius Caesar when he was a small boy.

JACK: What did the bald man say when he received a comb for his birthday?

TOM: I don't know, what did he say?

JACK: Thanks very much, I'll never part with it.

The census taker knocked on Miss Matty's door. She answered all his questions except one. She refused to tell him her age.

"But everybody tells their age to the census taker," he said.

"Did Miss Maisie Hill and Miss Daisy Hill tell you their ages?"

"Certainly."

"Well, I'm the same age as they are," she snapped.

"As old as the Hills," he wrote on his form.

POST OFFICE CLERK: Here's your stamp.

SHOPPER *(with arms full of packages)*: Do I have to stick it on myself?

POST OFFICE CLERK: No, on the envelope.

LITTLE GIRL: I was going to buy you some hankies for Christmas, Uncle, but I couldn't remember the size of your nose.

Young Larry and Barry were watching men on high scaffolding repairing a tall chimney.

"What would you do if you were up there and that thing fell?" Larry asked.

"I would wait until it got nearly to the ground and then I would jump."

HUSBAND (*phoning his wife from his office*): I've got two tickets for the ballet.

WIFE: Oh, lovely, I'll start getting ready.

HUSBAND: Yes, do—the tickets are for tomorrow night.

8

Give & Take

Bert had a letter from his mother.

"Dear Bert, so much has happened since you were home. I've had all my teeth out, and a new gas stove put in. . . ."

"Excuse me, can you tell me the time?"
"I'm sorry—I'm a stranger here myself."

TEACHER: What is a skeleton?
MARVIN: It's a man with his outsides off and his insides out.

TEACHER: I hope I didn't see you looking at someone else's paper, Jamie.
JAMIE: I hope so too.

"My uncle gets a warm reception wherever he goes."
"He must be very popular."
"No, he's a fireman."

What happened to the cat that swallowed a ball of wool?
She had mittens.

WILLY: What is frozen tea?
SAMMY: Iced tea.
WILLY: What is frozen juice?
SAMMY: Iced juice.
WILLY: What is frozen ink?
SAMMY: Iced ink.
WILLY: Well, go and have a bath.

DAN: This match won't light.
STAN: Why, what's the matter with it?
DAN: I don't know—it was all right a minute ago.

"I've made the chicken soup."
"Good—I was afraid it was for us."

MORRIS: I hear the workers in the mint are complaining about having too much work to do.
HARRIS: Yes, they're threatening to go out on strike unless they make less money.

FATHER: I'm worried about you always being at the bottom of your class.
FREDDIE: Don't worry, Dad. They teach the same thing at both ends.

"Where did I come from?" asked the baby ear of corn.
"The stalk brought you," answered its mother.

"I understand you buried your husband last week?"
"Yes, I had to; he was dead."

PRETTY GIRL *(at party to best-selling author)*: Oh, I've read all your books. The one I liked best was the one with the green leather cover and the gold lettering.

Overheard at the magicians' convention: "Hi, there, Terry, how's tricks?"

SMITH: You seem to have been working in your garden. Mr. Brown—what are you growing?
BROWN: Tired.

FRIEND: You should pay your taxes with a smile.

SMUG CITIZEN: Yes, I'd like to, but they insist on cash.

MOTHER: Eat your cabbage, dear, it will put color into your cheeks.

ANGIE: Who wants green cheeks?

"You can't help admiring our boss."

"Why is that?"

"If you don't—you're fired."

CUSTOMER: I'd like two pork chops, please, and make them lean.

BUTCHER: Yes, ma'am, which way?

The lady with the large flowery hat was stopped at the church door by the usher.

"Are you a friend of the bride?" he asked.

"Certainly not," shc snapped. "I'm the groom's mother."

"I think grandma needs new glasses."

"What makes you say that, son?"

"She's been watching two pairs of father's pants going around in the washing machine—and thinks she's watching a wrestling match on TV."

HENRY: This old bum came up to me and said he hadn't had a bite in two weeks.

BOB: Poor fellow—what did you do?

HENRY: Bit him, of course!

OFFICE MANAGER: I'm afraid that young man I hired isn't honest.

ACCOUNTS CLERK: Oh, you shouldn't judge by appearances.

OFFICE MANAGER: I'm not—I'm judging by disappearances!

GEORGE: I see you're still on crutches, old man.

LEON: Yes—that's the last time I'll try and jump over the net at table tennis.

"What's a girl like you doing in a nice place like this?"

BARBER *(to youth with slick, plastered-down hair)*: Do you just want me to cut it or would you like an oil check, too?

MRS. WHITE: Where are you living now, Mrs. Green?

MRS. GREEN: Just by the river. Drop in some time.

"Oh, Doctor, I swallowed the film out of my camera!"

"Well, we'll just have to hope that nothing develops."

SIMON: Which side of the bed do you sleep on?
DOPEY DAN: The top side, of course.

DOUG: What do you think happened to the plant in our arithmetic class?
DICK: I don't know, what?
DOUG: It grew square roots.

TAILOR: Your suit will be ready in two months, sir.
CUSTOMER: Two months! It only took six days when God made the world.
TAILOR: True, sir, but look at the state the world is in.

MAUD: Samantha reminds me of a film star.
IVY: Really—which one?
MAUD: Lassie.

VOICE *(on phone)*: Is Mr. Miller in yet?
SECRETARY: No, he hasn't even been in yesterday yet.

FATHER: What's that gash on your forehead?
SILLY SON: I bit myself.
FATHER: How on earth could you do that?
SILLY SON: I stood on a chair.

TEACHER: Wendy, say a sentence beginning with "I."
WENDY: "I is . . ."
TEACHER: No, Wendy, you must say, "I am."
WENDY: All right, "I am the ninth letter of the alphabet."

TEACHER: You know that Russell boy?
PRINCIPAL: What about him?
TEACHER: Not onply is he the worst-behaved child in the school, but he has a perfect attendance record.

SALESMAN: Would you like to try our new oatmeal soap?
CUSTOMER: No, thank you, I never wash my oatmeal.

PATIENT: I always feel that I'm covered in gold paint, Doctor.
PSYCHIATRIST: Oh, that's just your gilt complex.

"Waiter, this coffee tastes like mud."
"Well, sir, it was ground only five minutes ago."

"I think I've got measles."
"That's a rash thing to say."

"Why don't you answer the telephone?"
"It's not ringing."
"Oh, you always have to leave everything till the last minute."

The muddled old gentleman went up to another man at the conference.

"I hardly recognized you," he said. "You've changed so much: your hair is different, you seem shorter, you've done away with your glasses. What's happened to you, Mr. Frost?"

"But I'm not Mr. Frost."

"Amazing—you've even changed your name!"

"And how do you like the meatballs?"
"I don't know—I've never been to any."

Little Diana was standing in front of her mirror with her eyes closed.

"Why are you standing there with your eyes closed?" asked her brother.

"So I can see what I look like when I'm asleep," she replied.

JULIE: That boy's annoying me.
WENDY: Why, he's not even looking at you.
JULIE: I know, that's what's annoying me.

CLAIRE: I see you're invited to Sandra's party.
ZELDA: Yes, but I can't go. The invitation says four to seven, and I'm eight.

THIEF: Quick!. The police are coming. Jump out of the window!
ACCOMPLICE: But we're on the thirteenth floor!
THIEF: This is no time to be superstitious.

9

Show & Tell

A woman went to visit a friend and carried a small box with holes punched in the top.

“What’s in your box?” asked the friend.

“A cat,” said the woman. “You see I’ve been dreaming about mice at night and I’m so scared! The cat is to catch them.”

“But the mice are only imaginary,” said the friend.

“So is the cat,” whispered the woman.

MAN *(in restaurant)*: Excuse me, waiter, how long have you been working here?
WAITER: About two months, sir.
MAN: Oh, then it couldn't have been you who took my order.

I stayed on a farm and one day a chicken died, so we had roast chicken. The next day a pig died and we had pork chops. The following day the farmer died—so I left.

ERIC: I've been asked to get married hundreds of times.
GLORIA *(surprised)*: By whom?
ERIC: My parents.

"Do you sell dog's meat?"
"Only if they come in with their owners."

MOTHER: Shall I put the kettle on?
FATHER: No, dear, I don't think it would suit you.

MOLLY: That's a nice suit you're wearing.
HARRY: Oh, do you like it?
MOLLY: Yes, who went for the fitting?

STUDENT: Did you say you learned to play the violin in six easy lessons?
MASTER: That's right. It was the seven hundred that came afterward that were the hard ones.

GIRL *(standing in the middle of a busy road)*: Officer, can you tell me the fastest way to get to the hospital?
POLICEMAN: Just stay right where you are.

RUPERT: How many dead people are there in a cemetery?
ROBERT: All of them.

LITTLE DIANA: Can you stand on your head?
LULU: No, I can't get my feet high enough.

VIC: I've changed my mind.
DICK: Thank goodness. Does the new one work any better?

"Charlie," called out the news editor to his reporter, "did you get that story about the man who sings tenor and baritone at the same time?"

"There's no story, sir," said the reporter. "The man has two heads."

YOUNG FISHERMAN: Is this a good river for fish?

OLD FISHERMAN: It must be, I can't get any of them to come out.

Two ladies met after a long time.

MRS. HUGHES: I believe your son is a very good football player. What position does he play?

MRS. EVANS: Oh, I believe he's one of the drawbacks.

LESLIE: Did your mother go in for weight lifting?

WESLEY: No, why?

LESLIE: Well, how did she ever raise a dumbbell like you?

MAYOR *(to visitor)*: What do you think of our town band?

VISITOR: I think it ought to be.

MAYOR *(puzzled)*: Ought to be what?

VISITOR: Banned.

The income tax expert was visiting the school to talk about taxes. "I'm going to tell you now about *indirect* taxes. Can anybody tell me what an indirect tax is?"

"A dog license," said Smart Alec.

"Why is that?" asked the expert.

"The dog doesn't pay it."

AUNTIE: Well, Billy, how do you like school?
BILLY: Closed.

VIC: She sure gave you a dirty look.
DICK: Who?
VIC: Mother Nature!

"Did you hear the one about the piece of rope?"
"No."
"Aw, skip it."

PATIENT: Doctor, do you think lemons are healthy?
DOCTOR: Well, I've never heard one complain.

ROSIE: This ointment makes my leg smart.
ROB: Well, why not rub some on your head!

BERNIE: Dad, would you do my arithmetic for me?
DAD: No, son, it wouldn't be right.
BERNIE: Well, at least you could try.

Mr. Briggs was making a knotty pine bookcase.

His young son pointed to it and said, "What are those holes for?"

"They're *knot* holes," replied his father.

"Well," said the lad, "if they're not holes, what are they?"

MOTHER: Where are you off to, Hubert?
HUBERT: I'm going to watch a solar eclipse.
MOTHER: All right, dear, but don't get too close.

PRISON OFFICER: Sir, I have to report that ten prisoners have broken out.
WARDEN: Blow the whistles, sound the alarms, alert the police—
PRISON OFFICER: Shouldn't we call the doctor first? It looks as if it might be the measles.

The office manager looked toward his assistant who was reading a magazine.

"Mr. Bright," he said, "I'd like to compliment you on your work—but when are you going to do any?"

Tim at boarding school sent this telegram to his father asking for money: "No mon, no fun, your son."

Back came the reply: "How sad, too bad, your dad."

RONALD: My wife's a kleptomaniac.
DONALD: Is she taking anything for it?

DWAYNE: Mommy, why do you have so much gray hair?
MOMMY: I expect it's because you are so naughty and cause me so much worry.
DWAYNE: Oh—you must have been terrible to Grandma!

After the telephone was installed in her home, the woman called the operator.

"My telephone cord is too long," she said. "Would you please pull it a little from your end?"

PAM: You see, Doctor, I'm always dizzy for half an hour after I get up in the morning.

DOCTOR: Well, try getting up half an hour later.

WORRIED PASSENGER: Captain, do ships this size sink very often?

CAPTAIN: No, ma'am, never more than once.

REGGIE: I'm going to buy a farm two miles long and a half inch wide.

ROGER: What would you grow on a farm that size?

REGGIE: Spaghetti.

JED: Why did the pioneers go west in covered wagons?

NED: I suppose they didn't want to wait forty years for a train.

In the attic, Gloria found an old family Bible. When she opened it, a large pressed leaf fell out.

"Aha!" she said, "Adam must have left his clothes here."

STEVE: How did you get that black eye?
STAN: I got hit by a guided muscle.

TEACHER: Sammy, what is water?
SAMMY: Water is a colorless liquid that turns black when I put my hands in it.

10

Crazier & Crazier

Two men sat next to each other in the doctor's waiting room.

"I'm aching from arthritis," said one.

"I'm Bent from Birmingham," said the other.

"Glad to meet you."

JACK: My uncle swallowed a frog.
JILL: Goodness, did it make him sick?
JACK: Sick! He's liable to croak any minute!

BRIGGS: My uncle disappeared when he was on safari.

BRAGG: What happened to him?

BRIGGS: My dad says something he disagreed with ate him.

DORIS: Why do they put telephone wires so high?

MORRIS: To keep up the conversation.

BUCK: I saw you pushing your bike to work this morning.

BEN: Yes, I was so late I didn't have time to get on it.

JESSICA: Is it correct to say that you water your horse?

MOTHER: Yes, dear.

JESSICA: Then I'm going to milk my cat.

TILLY: Why did the germ cross the microscope?

BILLY: To get to the other slide.

MOTHER: I've told you a million times not to exaggerate.

FATHER: Where did your mother go?
SON: She's round at the front.
FATHER: I know what she looks like, I want to know where she is.

DAN: My kid brother thought a football coach had four wheels.
STAN: How many does it have?

CALLER *(at door)*: Do you believe in the hereafter, ma'am?
WOMAN: Yes.
CALLER: Well, I'm the landlord, and I'm here after the rent.

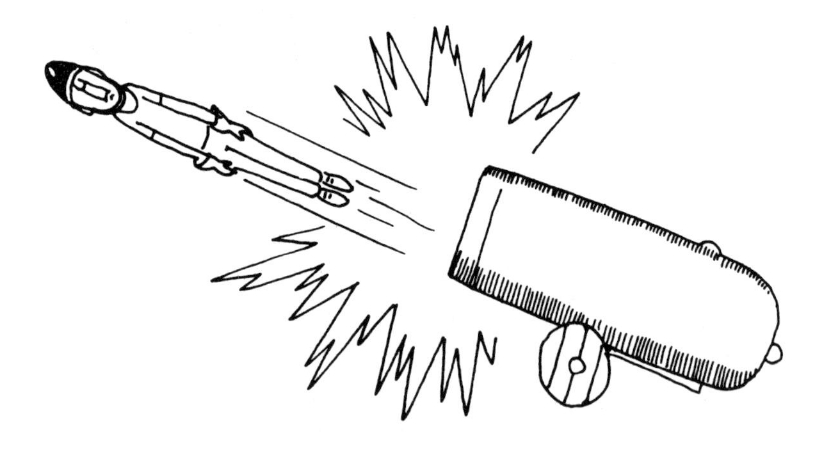

BERYL: What happened to the human cannonball at the circus?
CHERYL: He got fired.

EVE: How old is your brother?
STEVE: He's a year old.
EVE: Well, I've got a dog that's a year old, and he can walk twice as far as your brother.
STEVE: He's got twice as many legs.

CUSTOMER: Waiter, I don't like all the flies in here.
WAITER: Well, just point out the ones you don't like and I'll have them put out.

FATHER: Who gave you that black eye?
JACK: Nobody—I had to fight for it.

LEE: What can run across the floor, but has no legs?
DEE: Water.

AUNTIE: Come on, Billy, dear, eat your cabbage, it's good for growing children.

BILLY: I don't want to grow any children.

DOCTOR: You need glasses.

PATIENT: How can you tell?

DOCTOR: I knew as soon as you came in the window.

MILLY: What are you writing?

MOLLY: I'm writing a letter to myself.

MILLY: What does it say?

MOLLY: How do I know—I won't get it 'til tomorrow.

MOTHER: Tommy, did you fall down with your good pants on?

TOMMY: Yes, Mom, I didn't have time to take them off.

NOAH *(to his son Ham, who is fishing)*: Go easy on the bait; remember I've only got two worms.

ANGIE: Why do storks lift only one leg?
GEORGIE: If they lifted the other leg they'd fall over.

MRS. GRAY: My husband beats me up every morning.
MRS. DAY: How terrible!
MRS. GRAY: Yes, he gets up at seven and I get up at eight.

PAT: How did you manage to crash your car?
MATT: You see that ditch over there?
PAT: Yes.
MATT: Well, I didn't.

Learn from the mistakes of others—you can't live long enough to make them all yourself.

POLICEMAN: I'm afraid I'm going to lock you up for the night.
HOOLIGAN: Why—what's the charge?
POLICEMAN: Oh, there's no charge—it's all part of the service.

DINER: Waiter, this meat isn't fit for a pig.
WAITER: I'll take it back, sir, and bring you some that is.

FANNY *(shaking her husband)*: Manny, I heard a mouse squeak.
MANNY: What do you want me to do—oil it?

HOTEL MANAGER: Well, sir, did you enjoy your stay with us?
GUEST: Yes, but it's hard leaving the place so soon after buying it.

WYNN: Whenever I'm down in the dumps, I buy new clothes.
LEN: So that's where you get them!

TED: Did you say your dog's bark was worse than his bite?
NED: Yes.
TED: Then, for heaven's sake, don't let him bark; he just bit me!

CHARLIE: Why does it rain, Dad?
DAD: To make the grass and the flowers grow.
CHARLIE: Well, why does it rain on the pavement?

MOLLY: Have you heard the latest? It's all over the building!
MILLY: What's all over the building?
MOLLY: The roof.

DORIS: Now that we're engaged, I hope you'll give me a ring.
HORACE: Of course, what's your number?

POLICEMAN: Here—why are you trying to cross the road in this dangerous place? There's a zebra crossing just a few yards up the road.
PEDESTRIAN: Well, I hope he's having better luck than I am.

MAVIS: Does your cat have fleas?
TOOTS: Don't be silly, cats don't have fleas; they have kittens.

KEITH: Don't you think I sing with feeling?
MAISIE: No—if you had any feeling, you wouldn't sing.

PATIENT: You were right when you said you'd have me on my feet and walking in no time.
DOCTOR: That's good; when did you start walking?
PATIENT: When I got your bill. I had to sell my car to pay it.

GRACIE: The trouble with you is you're always wishing for something you don't have.
TOM: What else is there to wish for

NEIGHBOR: Your daughter is only four and can spell her name backward? What's her name?
PROUD MOTHER: Ada.

VISITOR TO FARM: Do you know how long cows should be milked?

FARMER: The same as short ones.

The bus was crowded, and as one more man tried to get on, the passengers wouldn't let him board.

"It's too crowded," they shouted. "Who do you think you are?"

"I'm the driver." he said.

FRAN: My sister is black and blue because she puts on cold cream, face cream, wrinkle cream, vanishing cream, hair cream, and skin cream every night.

RHODA: But why does that make her black and blue?

FRAN: She keeps slipping out of bed.

SIDNEY: Show me a tough guy and I'll show you a coward.

SAM: Well, I'm a tough guy.

SIDNEY: I'm a coward.

11

Look Out!

In the snake house at the zoo, one snake said to another, "Are we supposed to be poisonous?"

"Why?"

"Well, I just bit my lip."

ROGER: Oh, he's a friendly dog! He'll eat off your hand.

LODGER: That's what I'm afraid of.

AUNTIE: Well, Gordon, suppose there were only two pieces of cake left—a large piece and a small one. Which piece would you give to your brother?
GORDON: Do you mean my big brother or my little one?

EFFIE: I've just swallowed a bone.
MOTHER: Are you choking?
EFFIE: No, I'm serious.

Goofy Gus had a rope hanging from a tree outside his window.

"What's that for?" asked his brother.

"It's my weather forecaster," said Gus. "When it moves, it's windy, and when it's wet, it's raining."

SHOP OWNER: Yes, ma'am, these are the same pork pies we've had for years.
CUSTOMER: Could you show me some you've made more recently, please?

JACKSON: There's one word that describes my wife—temperamental.
JONES: In what way?
JACKSON: She's fifty percent temper and fifty percent mental!

The trumpet player had been blasting away all day, when there was a knock on his door.

"I live next door to you," he explained. "Do you know I work nights?"

"No," said the trumpet player, "but if you hum a few bars, I'll get the melody."

JOHN: Why is Sunday the strongest day?
JOAN: Because all the others are weekdays.

STAN: What are you taking for your cold?
SID: What will you give me?

Visiting the modern art museum, a woman turned to an attendant standing nearby.

"This," she said, "I suppose, is one of those hideous representations you call modern art?"

"No, ma'am," replied the attendant. "That one's called a mirror."

Think of a number between one and twenty. Double it, subtract eighteen, add one, subtract the number you started with, close your eyes. . . . Dark, isn't it!

TEACHER: Yes, Theodore, what is it?

THEODORE: I don't want to alarm you, Miss Bates, but my dad said if I didn't get better marks, someone was going to get a licking.

TEACHER: David, this is the fifth day this week you've had to stay in after school. What have you to say for yourself?

DAVID: I'm certainly glad it's Friday.

AL: Why can't two elephants go into a swimming pool at the same time?

SAL: Because they have only one pair of trunks.

Dustin's mother was worried about the health of her neighbor.

"Dustin," she said, "run and ask how old Mrs. Jones is."

Soon Dustin was back. "Mrs. Jones was very annoyed," he said. "She said it was none of your business how old she is."

Hickory dickory dock—
Three mice ran up the clock—
The clock struck one—
But the other two managed to get away!

"Do you know how to make a slow horse fast?"
"No, do you?"
"Yes, don't give him anything to eat."

"Waiter, there's a twig in my soup."
"Just a moment, sir, I'll call the branch manager."

FRANK: What would I have to give you to get a little kiss?
ZAZA: Chloroform.

Have you heard the one about quicksand?
It takes a long time to sink in.

FRANK: Am I the first man you've ever kissed?
SUE: You might be—your face looks familiar.

"What are you eating, Sonny?"
"An apple."
"Better look out for worms."
"Let the worms look out for themselves."

DOCTOR: I'm sorry to have to tell you that you may have rabies, and it could prove fatal.

PATIENT: Well, Doctor, please give me a pencil and paper.

DOCTOR: To make your will?

PATIENT: No—to make a list of people I want to bite.

What did the traffic lights say to the sports car?

"Don't look now, I'm changing."

EFFIE: My aunt was very embarrassed when she was asked to take off her mask at the party.

TESSIE: Why was that?

EFFIE: She wasn't wearing one.

"How dare you spit in front of my wife?"
"Why, was it her turn?"

ANGRY MAN: I'll teach you to throw stones at my greenhouse.

LITTLE HORROR: I wish you would; I keep missing it.

"I've got a nasty pain in my right foot, Doctor."
"You shouldn't worry, it's just old age."
"Well, why doesn't the other one hurt, I've had that just as long?"

MONTY: Is it really bad luck to have a black cat follow you?
MIKE: Well, it depends on whether you're a man or a mouse.

LECTURER *(to chairman)*: May I sit on your right hand?
CHAIRMAN: You may—but I'll need it later to ring the bell.

Index